World Series Champions: Philadelphia Phillies

Third baseman Mike Schmidt

Pitcher Aaron Nola

WORLD SERIES CHAMPIONS

PHILADELPHIA PHILLIES

MICHAEL E. GOODMAN

CREATIVE EDUCATION / CREATIVE PAPERBACKS

Published by Creative Education and Creative Paperbacks
P.O. Box 227, Mankato, Minnesota 56002
Creative Education and Creative Paperbacks are imprints of
The Creative Company
www.thecreativecompany.us

Art Direction by Tom Morgan
Book production by Ciara Beitlich
Edited by Jae Tischler

Photographs by Alamy (Cal Sport Media, Don Senia Murray/Zuma
Press, Inc., UPI), Corbis (Dan Bigelow), Getty (David Banks, Robert
Leiter, Library of Congress, Jim McIsaac, Rich Pilling, Casey Sykes,
Rob Tringali/Sportschrome, UPI/Alamy Stock Photo)

Library of Congress Cataloging-in-Publication Data
Names: Goodman, Michael E., author.
Title: Philadelphia Phillies / Michael E. Goodman.
Description: Mankato, MN : Creative Education and Creative
    Paperbacks, [2024] | Series: Creative sports, World Series
    champions | Includes index. | Audience: Ages 7-10 | Audience:
    Grades 2-3 | Summary: "Elementary-level text and engaging
    sports photos highlight the Philadelphia Phillies' MLB World Series
    wins and losses, plus sensational players associated with the
    professional baseball team such as Bryce Harper."-- Provided by
    publisher.
Identifiers: LCCN 2023008201 (print) | LCCN 2023008202 (ebook)
    | ISBN 9781640268326 (library binding) | ISBN 9781682773826
    (paperback) | ISBN 9781640269859 (pdf)
Subjects: LCSH: Philadelphia Phillies (Baseball team)--History--
    Juvenile literature. | World Series (Baseball)--History--Juvenile
    literature.
Classification: LCC GV875.P45 G66 2024 (print) | LCC GV875.P45
    (ebook) | DDC 796.357/640974811--dc23/eng/20230223
LC record available at https://lccn.loc.gov/2023008201
LC ebook record available at https://lccn.loc.gov/2023008202

Printed in China

2008 World Series Champions

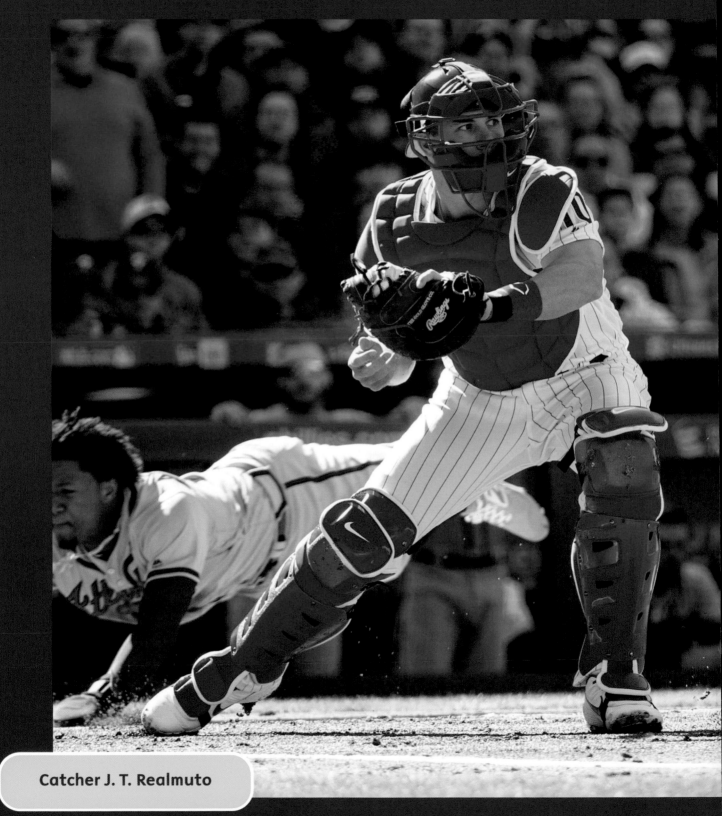

Catcher J. T. Realmuto

CONTENTS

Home of the Phillies

**P**hiladelphia, Pennsylvania, is a city full of U.S. history. It's the birthplace of the nation. It's where the Declaration of Independence was signed. Philadelphia is also rich in baseball history. The Phillies have been playing there since 1883. They play their home games at Citizens Bank Park. Fans at the **stadium** wear red hats with a big white P on the front.

The Philadelphia Phillies are a Major League Baseball (MLB) team. They are part of the National League (NL) East Division. Their biggest **rivals** are the New York Mets. All MLB teams try to win the World Series to become champions.

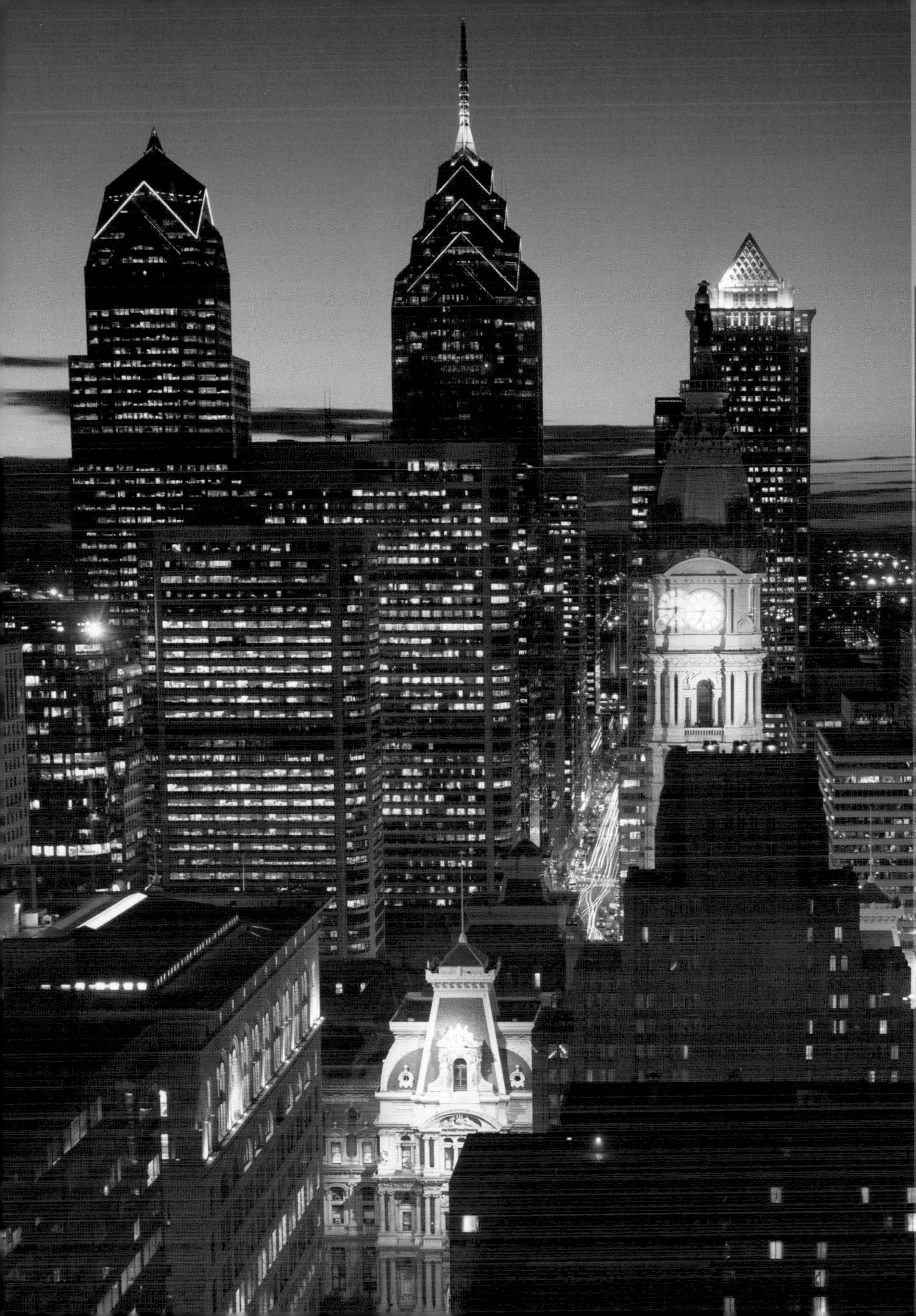

Pitcher Cole Hamels

Naming the Phillies

The team was first called the Quakers. In 1890, owner Alfred Leach decided to change the name to Phillies. "It tells you who we are and where we're from," he said. No other baseball team has had the same name as long as the Phillies.

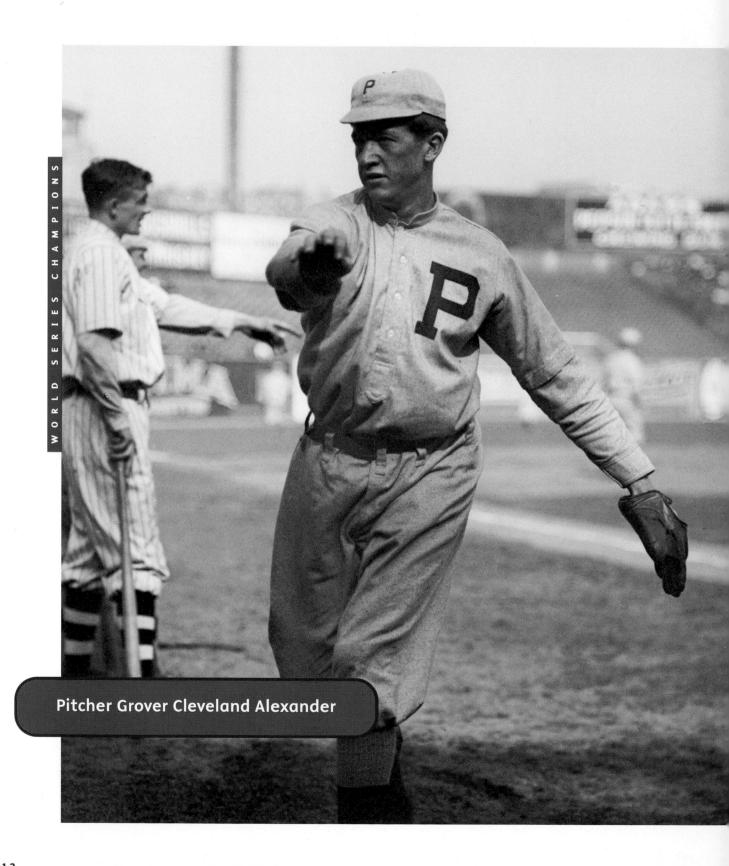

Pitcher Grover Cleveland Alexander

Phillies History

The Quakers won only 17 games their first season. They quickly got better. The Phillies captured their first NL **pennant** in 1915. But they lost in the World Series. The club's best player was pitcher Grover Cleveland Alexander. He won 31 games that year.

In 1950, the Phillies had a magical season. Fans called them the "Whiz Kids." Pitcher Robin Roberts won 20 games. He helped his team get to the World Series. But they lost to the New York Yankees.

The Phillies did not reach the World Series again until 1980. This time, they would not be stopped. Pitcher Steve "Lefty" Carlton won two series games. Third baseman Mike Schmidt pounded hit after hit. The Phillies were champions at last!

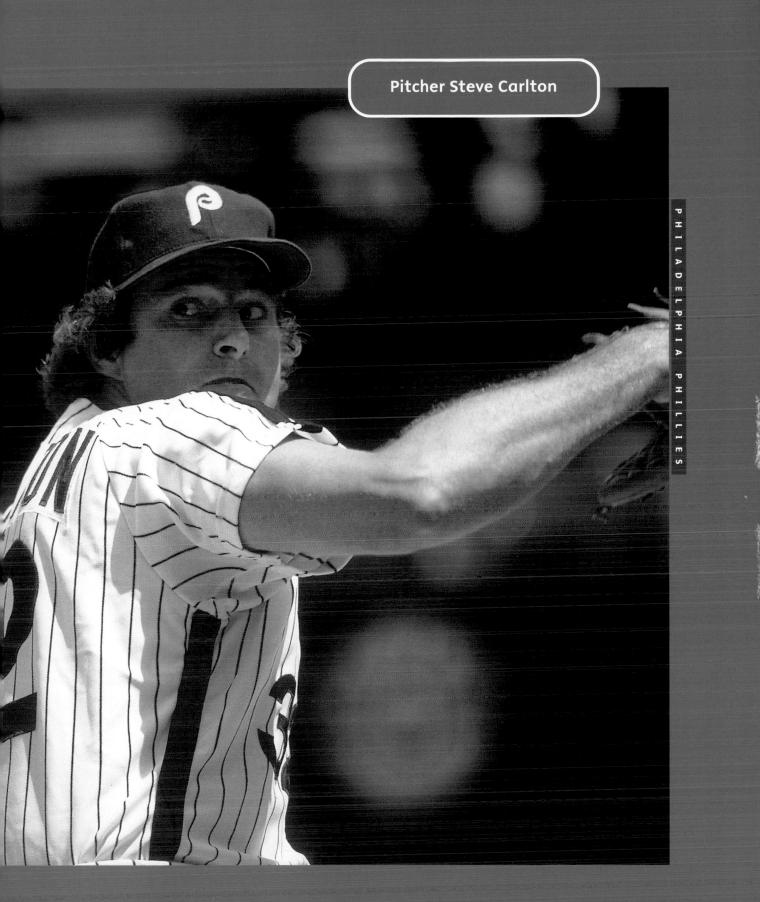

Pitcher Steve Carlton

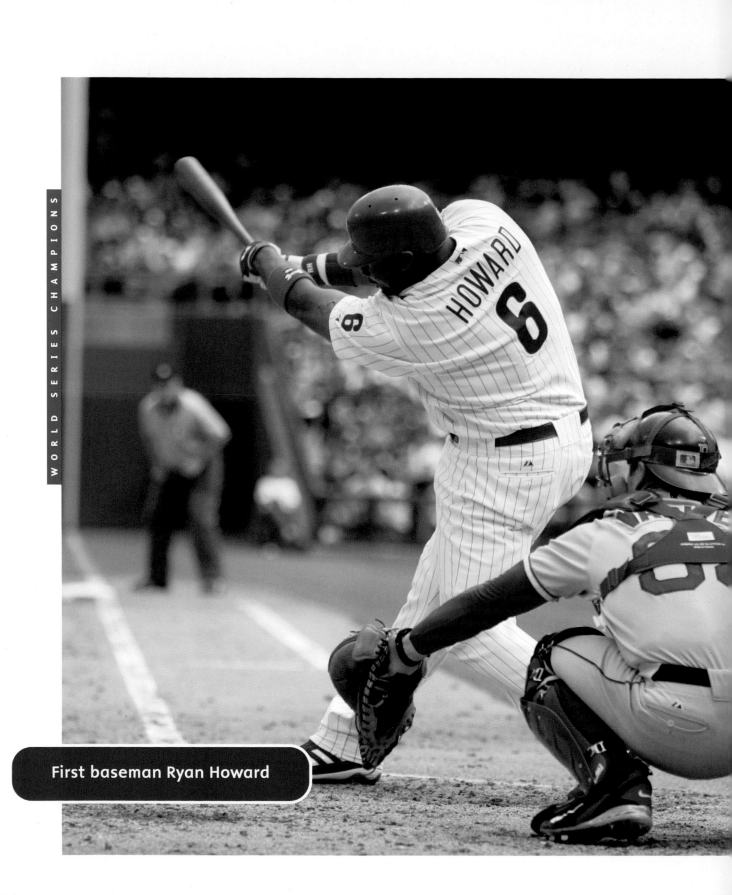

First baseman Ryan Howard

The Phillies earned a second **title** in 2008. First baseman Ryan Howard slammed three home runs. Cole Hamels threw curveballs that were hard to hit.

Philadelphia fans packed Citizens Bank for more World Series games in 2009 and 2022. Sadly, the Phillies came up short both times.

Other Phillies Stars

Outfielder Richie Ashburn was a batting and fielding star in the 1950s. He earned a place in the **Hall of Fame**. Later, he became a radio and TV announcer for the Phillies for 34 years.

Shortstop Jimmy Rollins played 15 seasons in Philadelphia. In 2007, he was named NL Most Valuable Player (MVP). He also won four Gold Gloves for his terrific fielding.

Shortstop Jimmy Rollins

Outfielder Bryce Harper

Outfielder Bryce Harper joined the Phillies in 2019. Two years later, he was named NL MVP. Fans are counting on him to bring another championship banner to Citizens Bank Park soon.

About the Phillies

Started playing: 1883

....

League/division: National
League, East Division

....

Team colors: red and blue

....

Home stadium: Citizens Bank Park

....

WORLD SERIES CHAMPIONSHIPS:

1980, 4 games to 2 over
Kansas City Royals

....

2008, 4 games to 1 over
Tampa Bay Rays

....

Philadelphia Phillies website:
www.mlb.com/phillies

....

Glossary

Hall of Fame—a museum in which the best players of all time are honored

. . . .

pennant—a league championship; a team that wins a pennant gets to play in the World Series

. . . .

rival—a team that plays extra hard against another team

. . . .

stadium—a building with tiers of seats for spectators

. . . .

title—another word for championship

. . . .

Second baseman Chase Utley

Index